Adult
MAD LIBS™

The world's greatest *party* game

Log On to Mad Libs

by Sean McMahill

PSS!
PRICE STERN SLOAN
An Imprint of Penguin Group (USA) Inc.

PRICE STERN SLOAN
Published by the Penguin Group
Penguin Group (USA) Inc., 375 Hudson Street, New York, New York 10014, USA
Penguin Group (Canada), 90 Eglinton Avenue East, Suite 700, Toronto, Ontario M4P 2Y3, Canada
(a division of Pearson Penguin Canada Inc.)
Penguin Books Ltd., 80 Strand, London WC2R 0RL, England
Penguin Group Ireland, 25 St. Stephen's Green, Dublin 2, Ireland
(a division of Penguin Books Ltd.)
Penguin Group (Australia), 250 Camberwell Road, Camberwell, Victoria 3124, Australia
(a division of Pearson Australia Group Pty. Ltd.)
Penguin Books India Pvt. Ltd., 11 Community Centre, Panchsheel Park, New Delhi—110 017, India
Penguin Group (NZ), 67 Apollo Drive, Rosedale, Auckland 0632, New Zealand
(a division of Pearson New Zealand Ltd.)
Penguin Books (South Africa) (Pty.) Ltd., 24 Sturdee Avenue,
Rosebank, Johannesburg 2196, South Africa

Penguin Books Ltd., Registered Offices: 80 Strand, London WC2R 0RL, England

Cover photograph © Photodisc/Digital Vision/Thinkstock

Published by Price Stern Sloan,
a division of Penguin Young Readers Group,
345 Hudson Street, New York, New York 10014.

ISBN 978-0-8431-7281-2
1 3 5 7 9 10 8 6 4 2

ALWAYS LEARNING   **PEARSON**

Adult MAD LIBS™ INSTRUCTIONS

The world's greatest _party_ game

MAD LIBS® is a game for people who don't like games!
It can be played by one, two, three, four, or forty.

• RIDICULOUSLY SIMPLE DIRECTIONS

In this tablet you will find stories containing blank spaces where words are left out.
One player, the READER, selects one of these stories. The READER does not tell
anyone what the story is about. Instead, he/she asks the other players, the WRITERS,
to give him/her words. These words are used to fill in the blank spaces in the story.

• TO PLAY

The READER asks each WRITER in turn to call out a word—an adjective or a noun
or whatever the space calls for—and uses them to fill in the blank spaces in the story.
The result is a MAD LIBS® game.

When the READER then reads the completed MAD LIBS® game to the other
players, they will discover that they have written a story that is fantastic, screamingly
funny, shocking, silly, crazy, or just plain dumb—depending upon which words each
WRITER called out.

• EXAMPLE (*Before* and *After*)

" _____ !" he said _____
     EXCLAMATION   ADVERB

as he jumped into his convertible _____ and
                                        NOUN

drove off with his _____ wife.
                        ADJECTIVE

"____ _Ouch_ ____ !" he said ____ _stupidly_ ____
     EXCLAMATION   ADVERB

as he jumped into his convertible ____ _cat_ ____ and
                                        NOUN

drove off with his ____ _brave_ ____ wife.
                        ADJECTIVE

In case you have forgotten what adjectives, adverbs, nouns, and verbs are, here is a quick review:

An **ADJECTIVE** describes something or somebody. _Lumpy_, _soft_, _ugly_, _messy_, and _short_ are adjectives.

An **ADVERB** tells how something is done. It modifies a verb and usually ends in "ly." _Modestly_, _stupidly_, _greedily_, and _carefully_ are adverbs.

A **NOUN** is the name of a person, place, or thing. _Sidewalk_, _umbrella_, _bridle_, _bathtub_, and _nose_ are nouns.

A **VERB** is an action word. _Run_, _pitch_, _jump_, and _swim_ are verbs. Put the verbs in past tense if the directions say **PAST TENSE**. _Ran_, _pitched_, _jumped_, and _swam_ are verbs in the past tense.

When we ask for **A PLACE**, we mean any sort of place: a country or city (_Spain_, _Cleveland_) or a room (_bathroom_, _kitchen_).

An **EXCLAMATION** or **SILLY WORD** is any sort of funny sound, _gasp_, _grunt_, or outcry, like _Wow!_, _Ouch!_, _Whomp!_, _Ick!_, and _Gadzooks!_

When we ask for specific words, like a **NUMBER**, a **COLOR**, an **ANIMAL**, or a **PART OF THE BODY**, we mean a word that is one of those things, like _seven_, _blue_, _horse_, or _head_.

When we ask for a **PLURAL**, it means more than one. For example, _cat_ pluralized is _cats_.

MAD LIBS® is fun to play with friends, but you can also play it by yourself! To begin with, DO NOT look at the story on the page below. Fill in the blanks on this page with the words called for. Then, using the words you have selected, fill in the blank spaces in the story. Now you've created your own hilarious MAD LIBS® game!

ADJECTIVE _____

ADJECTIVE _____

PLURAL NOUN _____

ADJECTIVE _____

PART OF THE BODY _____

NOUN _____

NOUN _____

NOUN _____

ADVERB _____

ADJECTIVE _____

VERB (PAST TENSE) _____

ADJECTIVE _____

CELEBRITY _____

NOUN _____

Adult MAD LIBS

GETTING BREAKING NEWS FROM SOCIAL MEDIA

The world's greatest _party_ game

Today, many of us find out about _____ events as they happen,

ADJECTIVE

thanks to social media. From earthquakes and other _____

ADJECTIVE

disasters, to political _____ and celebrity deaths, we often get

PLURAL NOUN

the news from our friends first. In fact, sometimes it can even seem

a bit _____, with certain people angling to be the first to

ADJECTIVE

share a story on _____-book or post a "R.I.P." _____

PART OF THE BODY — NOUN

update. However, due to the nature of the _____ and hearing

NOUN

things second- and thirdhand, you can't always be sure that what

you're reading is the _____. Many celebrities' deaths have

NOUN

been _____ reported, whether from _____ information

ADVERB — ADJECTIVE

or as hoaxes. It's sort of like the twenty-first-century version of the

game Telephone. When Kim Jong-Il _____, many people

VERB (PAST TENSE)

began to ask how the _____ rapper Lil' Kim had died. Unless

ADJECTIVE

you're _____ friends with Anderson Cooper or Katie Couric, it

ADJECTIVE

might be best to consider the source next time you rush to tweet your

condolences to the family of _____ after they die in a freak

CELEBRITY

_____-climbing accident.

NOUN

Adult MAD LIBS™ FACEBOOK ETIQUETTE

The world's greatest _party_ game

MAD LIBS® is fun to play with friends, but you can also play it by yourself! To begin with, DO NOT look at the story on the page below. Fill in the blanks on this page with the words called for. Then, using the words you have selected, fill in the blank spaces in the story. Now you've created your own hilarious MAD LIBS® game!

VERB _____

NOUN _____

NOUN _____

PLURAL NOUN _____

ADJECTIVE _____

A PLACE _____

VERB ENDING IN "ING" _____

ADJECTIVE _____

ADJECTIVE _____

ARTICLE OF CLOTHING _____

PLURAL NOUN _____

ADJECTIVE _____

VERB _____

ADJECTIVE _____

PART OF THE BODY _____

When you _____ Facebook, you might be inundated with
VERB

notifications of recent activities: friends "liking" your _____,
NOUN

commenting on articles you've read on the _____ *Post*
NOUN

or _____ you've listened to on Spotify, or tagging you in
PLURAL NOUN

embarrassing photos of that _____ weekend you spent in (the)
ADJECTIVE

_____. Some people are compulsive likers, _____ every
A PLACE _VERB ENDING IN "ING"_

_____ thing you post. It can be difficult to tell who's just being
ADJECTIVE

_____ or who might be trying to get in your _____.
ADJECTIVE _ARTICLE OF CLOTHING_

You might also find yourself getting "poked." Now, some

_____ might view a poke as a friendly, _____
PLURAL NOUN _ADJECTIVE_

gesture, like a wave. Or maybe someone is trying to _____
VERB

your attention. Then again, it might have a more _____
ADJECTIVE

connotation . . . depends on what they're poking you with. After all, a

finger is one thing, but a/an _____ is another!
PART OF THE BODY

YOUTUBE CELEBRITIES

The world's greatest _party_ game

MAD LIBS® is fun to play with friends, but you can also play it by yourself! To begin with, DO NOT look at the story on the page below. Fill in the blanks on this page with the words called for. Then, using the words you have selected, fill in the blank spaces in the story. Now you've created your own hilarious MAD LIBS® game!

COLOR _____

PLURAL NOUN _____

PART OF THE BODY _____

VERB ENDING IN "ING" _____

VERB _____

ADJECTIVE _____

PLURAL NOUN _____

PLURAL NOUN _____

PLURAL NOUN _____

VERB _____

ADJECTIVE _____

ADJECTIVE _____

ADJECTIVE _____

PLURAL NOUN _____

NOUN _____

PART OF THE BODY _____

CELEBRITY _____

Adult MAD LIBS™ YOUTUBE CELEBRITIES

The world's greatest _party_ game

It's really easy to fall into a _____ hole of videos on YouTube.

COLOR

It can start with looking up _____ of your favorite singers or

PLURAL NOUN

old commercials for _____-paste or _____ gum. But

PART OF THE BODY VERB ENDING IN "ING"

there's also a world of original clips out there, videos that people

_____ on a/an _____ basis. They might be singing their

VERB ADJECTIVE

favorite _____ or giving tips on how to apply _____

PLURAL NOUN PLURAL NOUN

properly or doing impersonations of famous _____ . Some

PLURAL NOUN

users _____ their pets doing _____ tricks or their

VERB ADJECTIVE

kids saying _____ things. Some videos go viral, just because

ADJECTIVE

they're so _____ . It might be a newscaster who falls down

ADJECTIVE

after stomping a bucket of _____ or someone wearing a/an

PLURAL NOUN

_____ mask who hits their _____ and falls down or a

NOUN PART OF THE BODY

young boy or girl crying and saying to leave _____ alone.

CELEBRITY

ONLINE DATING

The world's greatest _party_ game

MAD LIBS® is fun to play with friends, but you can also play it by yourself! To begin with, DO NOT look at the story on the page below. Fill in the blanks on this page with the words called for. Then, using the words you have selected, fill in the blank spaces in the story. Now you've created your own hilarious MAD LIBS® game!

TYPE OF FOOD _____

ADJECTIVE _____

NOUN _____

VERB _____

NOUN _____

ADJECTIVE _____

PART OF THE BODY _____

ADJECTIVE _____

A PLACE _____

NOUN _____

PLURAL NOUN _____

VERB _____

ADJECTIVE _____

NOUN _____

ADJECTIVE _____

PART OF THE BODY _____

PLURAL NOUN _____

Meeting new people is easier than _____, thanks to the
TYPE OF FOOD

Internet and technology. Numerous _____ dating sites now
ADJECTIVE

exist, where you can try to find your soul _____, or at least
NOUN

_____ a date. You can specify the type of _____ you're
VERB   _NOUN_

looking for—age, gender, body type, _____ background,
ADJECTIVE

ethnicity, even the color of their _____. Sites will also try to
PART OF THE BODY

match you up with people who have the same _____ values
ADJECTIVE

as you do, like if you go to (the) _____ every Sunday or if
A PLACE

you vote as a Republican or as a/an _____. You might take a
NOUN

questionnaire and provide answers about how much you work out,

what your favorite _____ are, your ideal vacation spots, and
PLURAL NOUN

which side of the bed you _____ on. And now there are even
VERB

new GPS-based apps for your _____ phone that show you
ADJECTIVE

the other people in your area looking for a/an _____. Because
NOUN

sometimes, the most _____ measurement isn't the size of your
ADJECTIVE

_____, it's how many _____ away you are.
PART OF THE BODY   _PLURAL NOUN_

MAD LIBS® is fun to play with friends, but you can also play it by yourself! To begin with, DO NOT look at the story on the page below. Fill in the blanks on this page with the words called for. Then, using the words you have selected, fill in the blank spaces in the story. Now you've created your own hilarious MAD LIBS® game!

NOUN _____

VERB _____

NOUN _____

ADJECTIVE _____

PLURAL NOUN _____

PLURAL NOUN _____

ADJECTIVE _____

CELEBRITY _____

PERSON IN ROOM _____

PART OF THE BODY _____

PLURAL NOUN _____

PLURAL NOUN _____

ADJECTIVE _____

PLURAL NOUN _____

With Pinterest, I finally have a/an _____ online that reflects my
NOUN

aspirational lifestyle. I can _____ images of things that I like
VERB

and want more of in my life. I have a/an _____ that features
NOUN

my favorite places, _____ spots and restaurants where I've been,
ADJECTIVE

and _____ that I've always dreamed of visiting. I can share my
PLURAL NOUN

recent clothing purchases or a cute pair of _____ and other
PLURAL NOUN

_____ items that I'd love to add to my wardrobe. I can pin
ADJECTIVE

photos of people I admire, like _____ or _____. I can
CELEBRITY   PERSON IN ROOM

pin pictures of foods that make my _____ water or photos of
PART OF THE BODY

delicious _____ that I've baked myself. I can even share
PLURAL NOUN

_____ that I want to get for my kids. Basically, it's like the
PLURAL NOUN

_____ version of myself that I'd like to be and how I want
ADJECTIVE

_____ to see me—except that there aren't any actual photos of
PLURAL NOUN

me at all! Those, I save for Facebook.

From ADULT MAD LIBS™: Log On to Mad Libs • Copyright © 2012 by Price Stern Sloan, an imprint of Penguin Group (USA) Inc., 345 Hudson Street, New York, NY 10014.

MAD LIBS® is fun to play with friends, but you can also play it by yourself! To begin with, DO NOT look at the story on the page below. Fill in the blanks on this page with the words called for. Then, using the words you have selected, fill in the blank spaces in the story. Now you've created your own hilarious MAD LIBS® game!

ADJECTIVE _____

ADJECTIVE _____

PLURAL NOUN _____

NOUN _____

CELEBRITY _____

VERB (PAST TENSE) _____

PLURAL NOUN _____

ADJECTIVE _____

PLURAL NOUN _____

ADJECTIVE _____

ANIMAL _____

CELEBRITY _____

CELEBRITY _____

PERSON IN ROOM _____

PART OF THE BODY _____

Tumblr is a/an _____ new frontier online where you're never
ADJECTIVE

quite sure what you might see. People post _____ pictures that
ADJECTIVE

they've taken or images of famous _____ or animated GIF files
PLURAL NOUN

taken from a movie or a television _____. Some Tumblrs are
NOUN

dedicated to a specific theme, like science fiction or how dreamy

_____ is. You might follow a Tumblr that only posts songs that
CELEBRITY

were popular in the decade you were _____ or fan artwork
VERB (PAST TENSE)

based on _____ from your favorite movie. And there are also
PLURAL NOUN

some very sexy Tumblrs that feature everything from attractive

_____ celebrities to full-on amateur _____. It gets really
ADJECTIVE   PLURAL NOUN

_____ when you feed all of these different elements into your
ADJECTIVE

Dashboard. You could end up seeing five cute _____ videos,
ANIMAL

followed by a photo of _____ having a drink with _____,
CELEBRITY   CELEBRITY

followed by a nude photo of _____ grabbing their _____
PERSON IN ROOM   PART OF THE BODY

seductively. Sometimes it's best just to keep scrolling down.

Adult MAD LIBS
PUTTING THE TWIT IN TWITTER

The world's greatest _party_ game

MAD LIBS® is fun to play with friends, but you can also play it by yourself! To begin with, DO NOT look at the story on the page below. Fill in the blanks on this page with the words called for. Then, using the words you have selected, fill in the blank spaces in the story. Now you've created your own hilarious MAD LIBS® game!

NOUN _____

PLURAL NOUN _____

ADJECTIVE _____

PLURAL NOUN _____

PLURAL NOUN _____

NOUN _____

ADJECTIVE _____

PLURAL NOUN _____

ADJECTIVE _____

NUMBER _____

NOUN _____

NOUN _____

VERB (PAST TENSE) _____

NOUN _____

PART OF THE BODY _____

Adult MAD LIBS™

PUTTING THE TWIT IN TWITTER

The world's greatest _party_ game

Many celebrities have hopped on the Twitter _____ -wagon.
                                              NOUN

For some, it's a way to keep in touch with their _____ , while
                                                  PLURAL NOUN

for others, it's a way to demonstrate how clever and _____ they
                                                        ADJECTIVE

are, in 140 _____ or less. Some stars post only very polished
              PLURAL NOUN

_____ that seem promotional in nature and are likely posted by
PLURAL NOUN

their public-relations _____ or some _____ intern. But
                         NOUN   ADJECTIVE

more interesting are the _____ who don't censor themselves—
                           PLURAL NOUN

even when they should. For instance, it's never a/an _____ idea
                                                       ADJECTIVE

to announce that you're going to take a Percocet, or _____ ,
                                                        NUMBER

and then keep tweeting your every _____ for the next three
                                    NOUN

hours. Or to state an unpopular _____ about a political topic,
                                  NOUN

then try to delete it and pretend it never _____ . And worst of
                                             VERB (PAST TENSE)

all, if you're trying to send a private _____ to someone, be sure
                                          NOUN

you aren't posting it to your feed . . . especially if a photo of your

_____ is attached.
PART OF THE BODY

Adult MAD LIBS™ — FACEBOOK ADDICTION

The world's greatest _party_ game

MAD LIBS® is fun to play with friends, but you can also play it by yourself! To begin with, DO NOT look at the story on the page below. Fill in the blanks on this page with the words called for. Then, using the words you have selected, fill in the blank spaces in the story. Now you've created your own hilarious MAD LIBS® game!

VERB _____

PART OF THE BODY (PLURAL) _____

ADJECTIVE _____

NOUN _____

NOUN _____

NOUN _____

ADJECTIVE _____

PLURAL NOUN _____

NOUN _____

NOUN _____

ADJECTIVE _____

NOUN _____

VERB _____

NOUN _____

NOUN _____

VERB _____

When you wake up in the morning, what's the first thing you

_____? Do you brush your _____, or make a nice,
    VERB   PART OF THE BODY (PLURAL)

_____ pot of coffee? Or do you sit down at your _____
ADJECTIVE   NOUN

and log onto Facebook? Maybe you're just curious to see what's going

on in the _____. But if there's a/an _____ of urgency or
           NOUN   NOUN

a fear that you might have missed out on something, then you might

have a/an _____ problem. Here are a few _____ to help
         ADJECTIVE   PLURAL NOUN

determine whether you might be addicted.

- Do you update your _____ multiple times a/an _____?
              NOUN   NOUN

- Do you take _____ photos of your _____ just to post
          ADJECTIVE   NOUN

online?

- Do you check your phone every time you _____ a notification?
                               VERB

- Have you created a profile _____ for your baby or your cat?
                       NOUN

- Have you ever posted a/an _____ while sitting on the toilet?
                     NOUN

If you wanted to "like" any of the above, it might be time to _____
                                                              VERB

off the computer and pick up a book.

The world's greatest _party_ game

MAD LIBS® is fun to play with friends, but you can also play it by yourself! To begin with, DO NOT look at the story on the page below. Fill in the blanks on this page with the words called for. Then, using the words you have selected, fill in the blank spaces in the story. Now you've created your own hilarious MAD LIBS® game!

NUMBER _____

PLURAL NOUN _____

NOUN _____

ADJECTIVE _____

PLURAL NOUN _____

ADJECTIVE _____

VERB _____

PLURAL NOUN _____

PLURAL NOUN _____

ADJECTIVE _____

VERB _____

ADJECTIVE _____

PLURAL NOUN _____

PLURAL NOUN _____

NOUN _____

ARTICLE OF CLOTHING _____

Adult MAD LIBS™

MY DEAR OLD FRIENDSTER

The world's greatest _party_ game

_____ years ago, social networking was so much easier. There
   NUMBER

were really only two _____ : MySpace and Friendster.
                  PLURAL NOUN

Friendster was the easier of the two: All you had to do was upload a/an

_____ of yourself, fill out a few _____ questions about
  NOUN   ADJECTIVE

your likes and _____ , and connect with your friends. There
                PLURAL NOUN

wasn't much to do beyond that. Then came MySpace, the flashier,

more _____ sister. You could _____ up your page with
    ADJECTIVE   VERB

sparkly _____ and animated GIFs and post songs by your
       PLURAL NOUN

favorite _____ . If your photos were _____ enough, you
     PLURAL NOUN   ADJECTIVE

might get messages from people you didn't even _____ . Many
                              VERB

users tried to show how exciting and _____ they were by posting
                        ADJECTIVE

photos holding a bottle of _____ seductively or in various
                PLURAL NOUN

_____ of undress. Soon it became a popularity _____ ,
 PLURAL NOUN   NOUN

with people adding new friends at the drop of a hat . . . or, more

accurately, the drop of a/an _____ .
                    ARTICLE OF CLOTHING

Adult MAD LIBS — THE MAYOR OF FOURSQUARE

MAD LIBS® is fun to play with friends, but you can also play it by yourself! To begin with, DO NOT look at the story on the page below. Fill in the blanks on this page with the words called for. Then, using the words you have selected, fill in the blank spaces in the story. Now you've created your own hilarious MAD LIBS® game!

NOUN _____

NOUN _____

A PLACE _____

VERB _____

ADJECTIVE _____

NOUN _____

NUMBER _____

PERSON IN ROOM _____

PLURAL NOUN _____

ADJECTIVE _____

NOUN _____

VERB _____

PLURAL NOUN _____

VERB _____

NOUN _____

PART OF THE BODY _____

ADJECTIVE _____

NOUN _____

PLURAL NOUN _____

NOUN _____

Adult MAD LIBS™ THE MAYOR OF FOURSQUARE

The world's greatest _party_ game

Have you ever wanted to be the mayor? With foursquare, you can be!

Basically, the _____ who "checks in" the most often at any
                  NOUN

given _____ will be crowned the mayor of (the) _____.
          NOUN   A PLACE

You _____ points every time you check in. If it's a/an
         VERB

_____ place, or if you're the first _____ to check in there,
  ADJECTIVE   NOUN

then you earn _____ points. If you and your friend
                    NUMBER

_____ both check in to the same places, then you get bonus
PERSON IN ROOM

_____. Certain places will offer you a badge for checking into
PLURAL NOUN

a/an _____ event or on a specific _____ of the week.
       ADJECTIVE   NOUN

You can go back and _____ where you've been, add tips about
                          VERB

certain _____, or send a ping to your friends when you
          PLURAL NOUN

_____ in. But once you've been crowned the _____, you
  VERB   NOUN

better watch your _____! It's a/an _____ title to keep.
                   PART OF THE BODY   ADJECTIVE

You need check in over and over again, several times a/an _____,
                                                               NOUN

so that no one else steals the honor away from you. Then again, it's

easy to become mayor at some _____. For instance, I'm the
                                PLURAL NOUN

_____ of my bathroom!
   NOUN

MAD LIBS® is fun to play with friends, but you can also play it by yourself! To begin with, DO NOT look at the story on the page below. Fill in the blanks on this page with the words called for. Then, using the words you have selected, fill in the blank spaces in the story. Now you've created your own hilarious MAD LIBS® game!

ADJECTIVE _____

ADVERB _____

ADJECTIVE _____

PLURAL NOUN _____

PLURAL NOUN _____

VERB _____

NOUN _____

VERB _____

PLURAL NOUN _____

PART OF THE BODY _____

PLURAL NOUN _____

ADJECTIVE _____

PLURAL NOUN _____

NOUN _____

Anyone can be a photographer—all you need is a/an _____
ADJECTIVE

phone. With Instagram, you can _____ take a photo, and then
ADVERB

tweak it so that it looks just like a/an _____-fashioned
ADJECTIVE

photograph. You get to choose from a variety of _____ that
PLURAL NOUN

adjust the coloring of the image, and you can also use the Lux feature,

which enhances even the smallest of _____ . There's also the
PLURAL NOUN

Tilt-_____ feature, which makes whatever is shown in your
VERB

_____ look like an adorable miniature version of itself. Then,
NOUN

once you've selected how you want your photo to _____ , you
VERB

can share it with all of your _____ so they can see what a great
PLURAL NOUN

_____ you have for photocomposition! You can scroll through
PART OF THE BODY

a feed of photos that your friends have uploaded and even see

_____ that strangers have taken. It's almost like the
PLURAL NOUN

_____ version of finding a shoe box full of old _____ at
ADJECTIVE   PLURAL NOUN

your grandmother's _____ . Maybe that's where the "gram" in
NOUN

Instagram comes from!

Adult MAD LIBS™

GOOGLE+WHAT?

The world's greatest _party_ game

MAD LIBS® is fun to play with friends, but you can also play it by yourself! To begin with, DO NOT look at the story on the page below. Fill in the blanks on this page with the words called for. Then, using the words you have selected, fill in the blank spaces in the story. Now you've created your own hilarious MAD LIBS® game!

ADJECTIVE _____

NOUN _____

VERB _____

PLURAL NOUN _____

NOUN _____

ADJECTIVE _____

VERB _____

ADJECTIVE _____

PLURAL NOUN _____

NOUN _____

NUMBER _____

ADJECTIVE _____

PLURAL NOUN _____

When Google decided to get into the _____ networking game,
                                        ADJECTIVE

they made it an extension of their online _____ and called it
                                              NOUN

"Google _____." If you already had a Google Mail account, it
          VERB

was easy to expand your profile and start adding your friends into

_____. You can have a/an _____ for your close friends,
PLURAL NOUN   NOUN

one for _____ associates, and one for people you don't even
          ADJECTIVE

really like all that much. Then, when you share something in your

"Stream," you can _____ who gets to see it. You can also create
                      VERB

a "Hangout," which is a/an _____ chat with up to ten
                              ADJECTIVE

_____. If you like a/an _____ that a friend has shared,
PLURAL NOUN   NOUN

then you can click the + _____ button. While Google Plus was
                            NUMBER

initially very _____, these days, the only _____ you're
                  ADJECTIVE   PLURAL NOUN

likely to see clicking +1 for the site are those who work for Google!

Adult MAD LIBS™

ARE YOU LINKEDIN?

The world's greatest _party_ game

MAD LIBS® is fun to play with friends, but you can also play it by yourself! To begin with, DO NOT look at the story on the page below. Fill in the blanks on this page with the words called for. Then, using the words you have selected, fill in the blank spaces in the story. Now you've created your own hilarious MAD LIBS® game!

VERB ENDING IN "ING" _____

PLURAL NOUN _____

PLURAL NOUN _____

NOUN _____

NOUN _____

ADJECTIVE _____

PLURAL NOUN _____

PLURAL NOUN _____

ADJECTIVE _____

VERB (PAST TENSE) _____

ADJECTIVE _____

NOUN _____

ADJECTIVE _____

NOUN _____

Adult MAD LIBS™

ARE YOU LINKEDIN?

The world's greatest _party_ game

When I decide it's time to start _____ for a new job, I head to
                                    VERB ENDING IN "ING"

LinkedIn. That way I can see what my former colleagues are doing,

what _____ they're working at, and explore whether there
        PLURAL NOUN

might be any _____ that sound appealing to me. I've also
                PLURAL NOUN

added my friends so that my professional _____ is as large as
                                            NOUN

possible. This way, I have a better chance of knowing someone in

common with a potential _____ at a/an _____ company
                          NOUN   ADJECTIVE

where I might like to apply. Then, those _____ can click
                                          PLURAL NOUN

through to see all of the _____ listed on my résumé as well as
                            PLURAL NOUN

read the _____ reviews my supervisors have _____ for
          ADJECTIVE   VERB (PAST TENSE)

me. However, _____ impressions still count, so I need to
               ADJECTIVE

choose a flattering _____ of myself to post on my profile. It's
                      NOUN

important to look professional—I wouldn't want my future boss to

think that I'm a/an _____ _____!
                      ADJECTIVE   NOUN

Adult MAD LIBS™ YELP!

The world's greatest _party_ game

MAD LIBS® is fun to play with friends, but you can also play it by yourself! To begin with, DO NOT look at the story on the page below. Fill in the blanks on this page with the words called for. Then, using the words you have selected, fill in the blank spaces in the story. Now you've created your own hilarious MAD LIBS® game!

NOUN _____

NOUN _____

PLURAL NOUN _____

VERB _____

PLURAL NOUN _____

NOUN _____

ADJECTIVE _____

ADJECTIVE _____

NOUN _____

PLURAL NOUN _____

PLURAL NOUN _____

NOUN _____

VERB _____

ADJECTIVE _____

NOUN _____

When hearing about a new _____ that's opened, I always want

NOUN

to know what a/an _____ has to say about the place before I

NOUN

go. That's why I love Yelp. It used to be that people had nowhere to

offer their unsolicited _____ about what they liked or didn't

PLURAL NOUN

_____ . But now, all of those _____ can be found in one

VERB   PLURAL NOUN

place! That way, before I even leave my _____, I'll know if the

NOUN

chicken is likely to be _____ , if the waiters are _____ ,

ADJECTIVE   ADJECTIVE

or if the _____ dispenser is empty in the restroom. These are all

NOUN

very important _____ to keep in mind when choosing a

PLURAL NOUN

restaurant! I know that people find my _____ very helpful,

PLURAL NOUN

which is why I always post a/an _____ every time I

NOUN

_____ at a new restaurant. After all, I have very _____

VERB   ADJECTIVE

taste—which is more than I can say for the _____ I had last

NOUN

night!

MAD LIBS® is fun to play with friends, but you can also play it by yourself! To begin with, DO NOT look at the story on the page below. Fill in the blanks on this page with the words called for. Then, using the words you have selected, fill in the blank spaces in the story. Now you've created your own hilarious MAD LIBS® game!

PLURAL NOUN _____

ARTICLE OF CLOTHING _____

VERB ENDING IN "ING" _____

NOUN _____

NUMBER _____

NOUN _____

PLURAL NOUN _____

VERB _____

PLURAL NOUN _____

VERB _____

ADJECTIVE _____

NOUN _____

PART OF THE BODY _____

I'VE GOT A HUNCH

The world's greatest _party_ game

If I'm looking for something to purchase, like some new household

_____ or a/an _____, I could easily just go to one of my
　　PLURAL NOUN　　　　　　ARTICLE OF CLOTHING

favorite online stores and start _____. But I prefer to go onto
　　　　　　　　　　　　　　　　VERB ENDING IN "ING"

Hunch and see what comes up. All I have to do is select a/an

_____, start browsing, and rate the items on a scale of one to
　　NOUN

_____ stars. Then, the site uses a decision _____ to try
　　NUMBER　　　　　　　　　　　　　　　　　　　　　　　　NOUN

to predict what I'll think of new _____. The more items I
　　　　　　　　　　　　　　　　　PLURAL NOUN

_____, the better it gets at predicting what I might like,
　　VERB

whether it's songs, restaurants, or _____. I can also recommend
　　　　　　　　　　　　　　　　　　PLURAL NOUN

certain things that I _____, whether I think they're amazing or
　　　　　　　　　　　　VERB

_____. And it's fun to see what's predicted for me, even when
　　ADJECTIVE

it's way off _____. After all, just because I like flowers, it
　　　　　　　NOUN

doesn't mean I have a green _____!
　　　　　　　　　　　　　　PART OF THE BODY

MAD LIBS® is fun to play with friends, but you can also play it by yourself! To begin with, DO NOT look at the story on the page below. Fill in the blanks on this page with the words called for. Then, using the words you have selected, fill in the blank spaces in the story. Now you've created your own hilarious MAD LIBS® game!

VERB _____

PLURAL NOUN _____

NOUN _____

NOUN _____

ANIMAL _____

VERB _____

VERB _____

PLURAL NOUN _____

ADJECTIVE _____

ADJECTIVE _____

ADJECTIVE _____

PLURAL NOUN _____

Adult MAD LIBS

TAGGED, YOU'RE IT!

The world's greatest _party_ game

Facebook is great for keeping in touch with people you already

_____, but if you're looking to meet new _____, visit

VERB   PLURAL NOUN

Tagged. There, you can browse profiles and see who has visited your

_____, too. If you find interesting people, you can check out

NOUN

their photos and send them a/an _____. You can also purchase

                                             NOUN

gifts to give, like a virtual rose or a teddy _____. Another way

                                                     ANIMAL

to _____ new people is by playing games. You can buy and

      VERB

_____ other people as pets, or harvest _____ on your

VERB   PLURAL NOUN

own virtual farm, and find _____ people to help you. You can

                               ADJECTIVE

also watch fun and _____ videos or go into groups and chat

                             ADJECTIVE

with other people who have _____ interests. Because if there's

                                   ADJECTIVE

anyone you want to meet, it's someone with enough spare time to be

hanging out online, looking for new _____ just like you!

                                        PLURAL NOUN

Adult MAD LIBS™ GET GETGLUE

The world's greatest _party_ game

MAD LIBS® is fun to play with friends, but you can also play it by yourself! To begin with, DO NOT look at the story on the page below. Fill in the blanks on this page with the words called for. Then, using the words you have selected, fill in the blank spaces in the story. Now you've created your own hilarious MAD LIBS® game!

NOUN _____

VERB ENDING IN "ING" _____

NOUN _____

ADJECTIVE _____

PLURAL NOUN _____

VERB _____

PLURAL NOUN _____

NUMBER _____

ADJECTIVE _____

ADJECTIVE _____

NOUN _____

PLURAL NOUN _____

NOUN _____

PLURAL NOUN _____

The world's greatest _party_ game

For anyone whose interactions with friends are mostly based on

entertainment, GetGlue is the social _____ for you! You "check
                                        NOUN

in" to whatever form of entertainment you're _____, whether
                                               VERB ENDING IN "ING"

it's a TV _____, a movie, or a/an _____ artist. For
          NOUN   ADJECTIVE

instance, you can favorite Beyoncé, and tell all your _____ on
                                                       PLURAL NOUN

Facebook when you _____ to her _____. You can also
                   VERB   PLURAL NOUN

unlock stickers, which you earn after checking in _____ times.
                                                    NUMBER

If a friend is watching _____ Family, you can vote whether
                         ADJECTIVE

that's "cool" or " _____." You can also discuss your favorite
                   ADJECTIVE

_____ with other people who like the same _____ as you
NOUN   PLURAL NOUN

do. It's the perfect social _____ for people who don't really like
                             NOUN

to socialize with other _____!
                         PLURAL NOUN

Adult MAD LIBS™ INSTANT MESS

The world's greatest _party_ game

MAD LIBS® is fun to play with friends, but you can also play it by yourself! To begin with, DO NOT look at the story on the page below. Fill in the blanks on this page with the words called for. Then, using the words you have selected, fill in the blank spaces in the story. Now you've created your own hilarious MAD LIBS® game!

ADJECTIVE _____

NOUN _____

VERB _____

PLURAL NOUN _____

NOUN _____

ADJECTIVE _____

ADJECTIVE _____

PLURAL NOUN _____

VERB ENDING IN "ING" _____

NOUN _____

NOUN _____

NOUN _____

VERB _____

NOUN _____

VERB _____

Adult MAD LIBS™   INSTANT MESS

The world's greatest _party_ game

Instant messaging is one of the most _____ inventions of the
                                        ADJECTIVE

twentieth century. You used to have to pick up a/an _____ and
                                                      NOUN

call someone if you wanted to _____ with him. But now you
                                 VERB

can sit at your computer and chat with multiple _____ at once
                                                  PLURAL NOUN

without ever saying a/an _____ out loud. You can message
                          NOUN

someone on Facebook or Gchat with them or use good, _____-
                                                       ADJECTIVE

fashioned AOL or Yahoo _____ messenger. The only problem
                          ADJECTIVE

can be when you're trying to hold too many _____ at once. You
                                              PLURAL NOUN

might forget who you're _____ with or accidentally type a/an
                          VERB ENDING IN "ING"

_____ to one person in the wrong chat _____. And if
 NOUN   NOUN

you have the _____ on your computer turned all the way up,
                NOUN

all those sounds can _____ you crazy! Especially if you're at
                        VERB

work or trying to finish a/an _____. In these cases, it might be
                                NOUN

better just to pick up the phone and _____ them!
                                        VERB

Adult MAD LIBS™ HOLD ALL COMMENTS, PLEASE

The world's greatest _party_ game

MAD LIBS® is fun to play with friends, but you can also play it by yourself! To begin with, DO NOT look at the story on the page below. Fill in the blanks on this page with the words called for. Then, using the words you have selected, fill in the blank spaces in the story. Now you've created your own hilarious MAD LIBS® game!

ADJECTIVE _____

PLURAL NOUN _____

VERB _____

ADJECTIVE _____

NOUN _____

PLURAL NOUN _____

VERB _____

PLURAL NOUN _____

NUMBER _____

PLURAL NOUN _____

NOUN _____

ADJECTIVE _____

VERB ENDING IN "ING" _____

NOUN _____

NOUN _____

NOUN _____

Adult MAD LIBS™

HOLD ALL COMMENTS, PLEASE

The world's greatest _party_ game

Reading news articles online is as _____ as pie. All you have to
                                        ADJECTIVE

do is Google a topic, and you'll find dozens of _____ online to
                                                  PLURAL NOUN

_____, and they're usually free. But use caution when reading
VERB

the _____ comments that are posted underneath the
       ADJECTIVE

_____. Reading the _____ might cause you to question
NOUN   PLURAL NOUN

why you even bothered to _____ the original article in the first
                             VERB

place. The comment section is usually filled with _____ who
                                                     PLURAL NOUN

have decided to weigh in with their _____ cents. With
                                        NUMBER

anonymity on their _____, commenters feel free to say any
                       PLURAL NOUN

and every _____ that crosses their minds. They don't worry
             NOUN

about facts or whether their opinions might be considered insulting

or _____. And soon, commenters will start _____ at
      ADJECTIVE   VERB ENDING IN "ING"

each other, arguing back and forth like an old married _____.
                                                          NOUN

I think most commenters should be banned from using the

_____! But then again, you might disagree. Feel free to leave
NOUN

me a/an _____.
            NOUN

Adult MAD LIBS™ AN EVITE TO DISASTER

The world's greatest _party_ game

MAD LIBS® is fun to play with friends, but you can also play it by yourself! To begin with, DO NOT look at the story on the page below. Fill in the blanks on this page with the words called for. Then, using the words you have selected, fill in the blank spaces in the story. Now you've created your own hilarious MAD LIBS® game!

NOUN _____

ADJECTIVE _____

PLURAL NOUN _____

PART OF THE BODY _____

NOUN _____

NOUN _____

PLURAL NOUN _____

VERB ENDING IN "ING" _____

ADJECTIVE _____

ADJECTIVE _____

NOUN _____

ADJECTIVE _____

VERB _____

NOUN _____

NOUN _____

PLURAL NOUN _____

Adult MAD LIBS™
AN EVITE TO DISASTER

The world's greatest _party_ game

Once upon a/an _____ , you might have received a paper
              NOUN

invitation in the mail, asking you to attend a/an _____ party.
                                                    ADJECTIVE

But now, almost all invitations are sent and received online on

_____ like Evite and _____-book. Not only can you see
PLURAL NOUN   PART OF THE BODY

who else was invited to the _____ , but you can see who is
                             NOUN

coming to the _____ and who is not. Interactions with the
               NOUN

other _____ begin before the party even gets _____ .
      PLURAL NOUN   VERB ENDING IN "ING"

Many people will comment on how they're looking forward to the

event or how _____ they are. Others will offer _____
              ADJECTIVE   ADJECTIVE

excuses as to why they might not make it or ask if they can bring a/an

_____ . And then there are those _____ hosts who want
NOUN   ADJECTIVE

to keep everyone excited, so they send multiple updates about what

they plan to _____ for dinner or a special _____ they
             VERB   NOUN

have planned. By the time the _____ actually rolls around, you
                               NOUN

might feel like you've already had enough of some of these

_____ !
PLURAL NOUN

Adult MAD LIBS™ LOL MEMES

The world's greatest __party__ game

MAD LIBS® is fun to play with friends, but you can also play it by yourself! To begin with, DO NOT look at the story on the page below. Fill in the blanks on this page with the words called for. Then, using the words you have selected, fill in the blank spaces in the story. Now you've created your own hilarious MAD LIBS® game!

ADJECTIVE _____

ADJECTIVE _____

NOUN _____

VERB ENDING IN "ING" _____

NOUN _____

TYPE OF FOOD _____

ANIMAL _____

PERSON IN ROOM _____

NOUN _____

NOUN _____

ADJECTIVE _____

NOUN _____

PLURAL NOUN _____

NOUN _____

VERB _____

One of the _____ ways to get to know someone is to take a
                ADJECTIVE

look at which Internet memes she shares with you. From the

_____ days of the Dancing Baby, nothing clues you in to
   ADJECTIVE

someone's personality like a/an _____. Some people really like
                                   NOUN

cats, whether it's seeing Nyan Cat _____ through the air or
                                    VERB ENDING IN "ING"

Keyboard Cat playing the _____ or LOLcats asking, "I Can
                            NOUN

Has _____?" Other animals have achieved popularity as
      TYPE OF FOOD

memes, such as the Dramatic _____ or the animated
                               ANIMAL

adventures of _____ the Unicorn. Some people enjoy silly
              PERSON IN ROOM

songs, like "Chocolate _____" or "Peanut Butter _____
                          NOUN   NOUN

Time." Others prefer even nerdier references from _____
                                                    ADJECTIVE

games, such as the phrase, "All your _____ are belong to us."
                                       NOUN

And then there are the videos that you might wish you'd never

received, like "2 _____, 1 _____." Much like Double
                  PLURAL NOUN   NOUN

Rainbow guy, all you can ask is, "What does it _____?"
                                                VERB

Enjoy more ADULT MAD LIBS™ from

PSS!
PRICE STERN SLOAN